Make Money Online Entrepreneur Series:

Book 5

Driving Traffic
with
Organic SEO

KIP PIPER

http://www.kippiperbooks.com

ISBN: 1886522-15-4
ISBN-13: 978-1-886522-15-2

YOUR FREE GIFT...

Want a free book? Want access to more freebies and special offers through Amazon?

As a way of saying *thanks* for your purchase, I'm offering a free eBook that is only available to my customers. Right now, you can get a copy of my book: *"28-Day Small Business Profit Plan: The Quick Start Guide for Business Success"*. This book is not sold anywhere else and can only be found on my website.

Plus, you will learn how to get instant notification whenever there is a **new free book** or **special book bundles** through Amazon.

Get the details at my website: **www.KipPiperBooks.com**

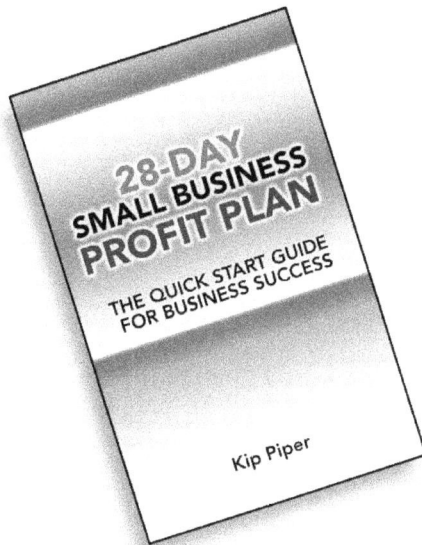

CONTENTS

AUTHOR'S NOTE

As you have probably experienced, the Internet and the websites on it are constantly changing. The information, examples, and screenshots presented in this book are accurate at the time of publication.

If you encounter any websites that have changed, please let me know by emailing me at: kip@kippiperbooks.com.

Remember, even though the website(s) may have changed, the principles, techniques and strategies in this book remain sound.

The links in this book are primarily affiliate links, which means if you purchase through the links, the price is the same to you and I receive a commission. This is the heart of affiliate marketing and entrepreneurship – which I am teaching you how to do with this book! I thank you in advance for using the affiliate links.

A FEW WORDS FROM KIP

Before I began teaching others how to blog and be successful with their online businesses, I wanted to be sure that I had something different to teach — strategies that are not easily found but can make a huge impact on success. The last thing I wanted to do is waste anyone's time. I wanted to offer something unique that would add both value and the potential for quick success for you.

Unknowingly, my research into online business success began in 1996 when I was first introduced to the concept of affiliate marketing. The potential for income excited me and I was quick to start experimenting with it. I joined Amazon.com and the few other affiliate programs available at the time. I added links on my website to products that related to my web design and Internet marketing business, with the purpose of offering quality resources to my website visitors and my clients. I encouraged and worked with my clients to include affiliate marketing in their overall online presence. I did this all in the hopes of adding to my income streams and eventually have affiliate marketing my dominant, if not sole, source of income.

But it did not come quickly, as others had promised or experienced. I totally, 100% believed in the concept of an online business and affiliate marketing (and still do), I understood the mechanics of setting up websites, creating products, and adding affiliate links, but I struggled with ranking my site high with the search engines and driving traffic to my site. Where were all the promised visitors who would buy what I offered or recommended so I could earn commissions?

Why were so many others achieving success? Why wasn't I experiencing the same success? Where was I going wrong?

I joined various mastermind groups. I purchased training programs from so-called "gurus". I bought books, read articles, watched videos, attended conference calls and webinars – I immersed myself in learning about blogging, affiliate marketing, and creating products.

The one most important thing I learned is that you need multiple websites, each focused on a different niche, to ensure a steady stream of income. "But," I asked, "if I can't get people to come to my first website, why should I spend more money and time creating websites that will not be visited either?" And each "guru" smiled nicely and said, "If you will upgrade your membership to our most expensive level, I'll tell you." But when I looked closely, I realized each "guru" was not living the life I wanted. In fact, most were working as hard or harder than I – with even less free time and income! They did not have the freedom of time and money that I wanted.

I didn't give up, though. I continued my search – knowing the one little "missing link" was out there.

One day I found it!

With this new knowledge, I knew without a doubt I could not only be personally successful with blogging, affiliate marketing and product creation, but now I could teach others those same strategies.

I realized that knowledge is what sets apart the training I offer – with this book and my other books which you can find at **http://www.kippiperbooks.com**.

This book is unique because it was written for *YOU*.

- YOU are someone who sees the potential in having an online business of affiliate marketing and product creation, but needs to know how to get started.
- YOU want practical strategies and advice that have already been tested and proven to work.
- YOU are ready for double-digit growth in sales.
- YOU are committed to following through with what you're about to learn.

This is why YOU are here.

Now please understand. Every piece of advice, strategy and practice has been tested on actual live blog, affiliate marketing and product websites – my own, my clients', and others. None of this is theory. You might then ask yourself, *ok, so how many blogs and affiliate websites has Kip done and what qualifies her as an "internet business expert"?* I think that's a great question. I wish more people questioned so called "experts" to see what qualifies them. As for me, I looked back on the last 15 years of stats and discovered that I have personally generated a 5-figure income in blogging, affiliate marketing and my own product sales – and that's just part-time!

If that's something you'd like to accomplish, you've selected the right book and series to begin with. I say "begin" because you'll soon discover that the learning process is a journey.

But don't worry! There's one more thing that qualifies me to lead you down this path – I'm just like you. It doesn't matter if you've never built a website or if you're already earning an income with blogging, affiliate marketing and your own product, and simply want to improve your sales. As you have already read, I've been wherever you are right now.

For anyone who reads this book and the entire *"Make Money Online Entrepreneur Series"*, and implements everything they learn, I can guarantee your business will move forward with more subscribers, sales and a stronger connection to your market. Like I said before, it doesn't matter if you've never built a website in your life or if you're already experienced, I've been there and can show you how to make blogging, affiliate marketing and product creation a successful income source.

But before we begin, I need you to do something. Connect with me on Facebook at:

http://www.facebook.com/TheRandomBlondeFanPage

I'd love to stay in touch and learn more about your journey.

You also are invited to check my website for more business books, and all of the books included in this *"Making Money Online Entrepreneur Series"*:

http://www.kippiperbooks.com

Thanks again for choosing to spend this time with me. Now let's get started!

"Done is better than Perfect!"

INTRODUCTION

This is Book 5 of the *"Make Money Online Entrepreneur Series"*: *"Driving Traffic with Organic SEO"*.

The entire series consists of more than 20 books, specifically written as an entire online business success training course.

Beginning in August 2013, I released one book a week, in the proper order to ensure success. If you follow the series from Book 1 to the end, one week per book, you will complete a 5+ month training course and master being an online entrepreneur! Of course, you can finish the series faster. Just make sure you fully complete the lessons in each book before moving on to the next. This way your success will be greater!

This series is carefully designed to give you every building block you need to build a successful online business. All of the guesswork is taken away, and by following this series, you will avoid most of the common mistakes made by new and even experienced online entrepreneurs. All is revealed – nothing is left out!

The beauty of this series is that you can pick up any book on whatever topic you need at this moment. Or you can purchase each book as it is released. Or ultimately, you can purchase the entire series in a bundle!

However you choose to use the information offered in this and the other books, you will be moving forward with intention and strategy for success in your business.

If at any time you have questions or desire personal one-on-one coaching for a particular topic, feel free to contact me at kip@kippiperbooks.com.

Here's to your online business success!

ONLINE BUSINESS SUCCESS CORE VALUES

Before we get started, it is important to understand, to be a successful online business entrepreneur, it is necessary that you stay focused on your business and have the core values that ensure that success. Here are the values that I have found to be essential to keeping focused and moving forward. These values will be at the beginning of every book of this *"Make Money Online Entrepreneur Series"*.

Be Passionate About Entrepreneurship

As it says, you need to be passionate about what you do and about being an entrepreneur. Being an entrepreneur will present the greatest challenges and the greatest joy you've ever experienced in the business world.

Commit 100% And GO FOR IT

One of the biggest things about being successful is being okay with putting yourself out there. Even if it's just a part-time business, commit 100% of yourself to the time you invest in your business. Commit to see it through and don't give up too soon. As the saying goes, "Don't give up before the miracle happens." Be patient and be persistent.

Build A Network of Support & influence

You must build a network of support and influence. This means building your Facebook community, building your Twitter community, and building your LinkedIn community. You must contribute to other people and help them be successful. By contributing to others and helping them be successful, you will become successful.

Get Comfortable with Being Uncomfortable

You're going to be doing a lot of things that you may or may not have done in the past. You can only grow when you're uncomfortable. When you're feeling comfortable and used to doing the things that you normally do, it's really difficult to grow, so you need to be comfortable with being uncomfortable see you can stretch and grow.

Consistent Growth & Improvement

It is important that you commit to consistent growth and improvement. We all need improvement especially if we are to grow and become successful, because staying up to date with the current tools and resources is essential. What helps you with consistent growth and continuing to improve is tracking your progress on irregular basis.

You also need to be okay with evaluating yourself and looking back at what you did and what you didn't do – without judgment. Simply observe and then recommit to the next step of growth and improvement.

80/20 Rule & Speed of Implementation

I'm sure you would've heard of the 80/20 rule (also known as Pareto's Rule) that 20% of what you do provides 80% of your success. So you need to understand that not everything you do is going to be perfect. Learn from it and move on. The quicker you get things done with the knowledge that you have, the more you'll be able to grow.

Flexible Persistence

Be persistent with everything that you do, and stay consistent with everything you do. The ones who experience the most success are the ones who are persistent in accomplishing their goals and are the most consistent in what they do. To be consistent, you must commit to regularly completing the tasks that ensure your success, whether those tasks occur daily, weekly, monthly, etc.

Surround Yourself With "A" Players

In business you deserve to surround yourself with the best and those who share your entrepreneurial spirit. You become like those you spend your time with. So choose carefully who you hang around with, so you are with those who think like you and make you stretch and reach higher.

The same goes for your employees. If you're going to outsource, you must select the best people who are competent and people you will enjoy working with. Avoid people who have negative attitudes. Surround yourself with those who embrace the concepts of small business success, entrepreneurship, and financial wealth.

Sell With Conviction

Be passionate about your product or service. Make sure you understand every aspect of it so that you can easily describe its features and benefits to your potential customers. If you have hesitations or doubts about your product, improve it so you don't have doubts.

Celebrate All Wins

Celebrate all victories! When you get that first sale, celebrate that first sale. Celebrate each new client. Celebrate each year of business success. Make sure you celebrate all wins. This is really important to maintain passion, momentum and to ensure success.

WHAT IS ORGANIC TRAFFIC?

Search engine optimization or SEO is all about accomplishing one goal, and that's getting ranked organically or capturing organic traffic.

So what is organic traffic?

Organic Traffic is simply when someone types a particular term or key phrase into Google or another search engine, and if your listing or website appears in the natural organic results, the traffic you generate from that is organic traffic! SEO or Search Engine Optimization is how we accomplish that goal.(Note: Organic Traffic is NOT to be confused with paid traffic.)

So let's take a 500-foot level-look at what organic traffic is and organic rankings are for the various search engines.

Organic Traffic Google

First is Google. Google is the "800-pound gorilla" in the search engine game. About 85% of all searches run on the Internet are run through Google's search engine. The image below has the Organic Results outlined:

Now, above the outlined organic traffic you see the Paid or Sponsored results and also on the right-hand side.

The Organic Results is what we talking about here as it pertains to Search Engine Optimization.

Organic Traffic Yahoo

Next is Yahoo organic results. As you can see from the image below, the layout is very similar to Google, where you have some advertisements on the top and the right, and the organic results is listed below:

Organic Traffic Bing

For the purposes of this book, lastly we'll take a look at Bing, which is Microsoft's own search engine. As you can see from the image below, again the layout is very similar – pretty much the same – to Google. The reason is Google is the biggest player, and Yahoo and Bing try to replicate what will is doing, with the paid advertisements on the top and the right, and the organic listings below.

Everything that we're going to discuss in this book as it pertains to SEO is how to get ranked organically.

Frankly, organic traffic is becoming more and more important, simply because people who are searching the web now have a greater understanding of exactly what are paid results versus organic results. Human nature always is to prefer or trust those organic, non-paid results.

So when websites aren't paying to be seen – they're not sponsoring or not paying for advertisement – people who use the search engines recognize the organic results as being more relevant. In addition, those organic results are, not only clicked on a lot more often, but the conversions once people visit the websites are typically much higher than paid or sponsored results. This is because people know that they came from an organic listing over a paid listing.

ORGANIC VS. PAID TRAFFIC

In this chapter, we're going to discuss the difference between organic traffic and pay traffic. Not only are we going to talk about the differences in the display of the search results, but more importantly we're going to take a detailed look at exactly the difference in traffic numbers and the amount of times these different results are being clicked in the search engines.

Paid or "Sponsored" Advertisements

So first let's take a look at the difference between organic and paid listings as it pertains to the amount of traffic to each of these different results.

Paid advertisements in Google appear on the top and on the right-hand side, as seen in the image below.

The truth is the paid advertisements on the top account for about 2-3% of the Total Search Traffic. So, for example, if 100 people search "funky baby clothes", only 2 to 3 people will click one of those top three paid advertisements.

Those on the right-hand side drop to about 1 to 2% of the Total Search Traffic. So using the same example as above, if 100 people search " funky baby clothes", only 1 to 2 people will click on one of the right-hand side paid advertisements.

Now these are rough numbers, but a good indication of typical traffic to paid advertisements. Another way to look at it is, anytime someone runs a search using the Google search engine, about 5% of the overall clicks go to the paid advertisements.

Some people might think, "Why would that be the case?" Especially when you consider that paid listings are at the top and the right, probably two of the most prominent locations on a page. Why are they getting such low traffic?

It hasn't always been the case. The traffic numbers have been coming down over time. The primary reason for only 5% of the clicks going to paid listings are simply because people who are searching in the Internet are becoming much more savvy. They're used to Google search rankings. People understand that when they click on a paid or sponsored result, they're going to paid or sponsored listings or websites that advertisers are paying for that position. It's human nature that people trust a third party or an organically generated result over a paid/sponsored listing. As you can see from a Total Search Traffic numbers above, this has been proven time and time again.

That's why the primary reason that paid results are only getting about 5% of the overall traffic. This really is a general rule, and this applies to almost all of the general searches.

First Organic Search Result

Referencing the Google image below, when we look a little bit deeper at the first organic search result (in dark red) that's listed below the top paid advertisements is going to count for 41-45% of the overall search traffic. This means, that for every 100 people who go and enter a search term into Google, 41-45 of those people will click on the first organic result. That is immensely powerful! So roughly one-half of the people that conduct a search are going click on that first organic listing. That is why being "Number 1 in Google" is so powerful!

Second Organic Search Result

The second result (in bright red) gets 11-18% of all search traffic. So for every 100 people that go and enter a search term on Google, 11-18 people will click that second organic result.

Third Organic Search Result

The third result (in orange) gets 7-15% of all search traffic or 7-15 people out of that hundred.

Fourth to Ninth Organic Search Result

The number four to nine organic results (in yellow) are going to get about 2% of the overall search traffic. If you're somewhere in that middle, you're going get about 2% of the traffic or 2 clicks for every 100 people that search that term.

Tenth Organic Search Result

If you're in tenth position (in green), you're going to get about 3-4% of overall search traffic.

Why does the tenth position get 2 to 3 times the traffic over positions 4 through 9? It's actually pretty simple. Every search result that Google returns will return 10 organic search results. What happens is people will search the listings, and not finding really anything that they really want, they get all the way to the bottom and they see that there's nothing left beyond 10. They really don't like to take the time or energy to go to a second, third or subsequent pages. So they just click the tenth organic search result. That's why the position 10 gets more traffic than 4 through 9.

As mentioned above, here is an image that shows how the Google first page organic traffic versus paid advertisements areas are laid out:

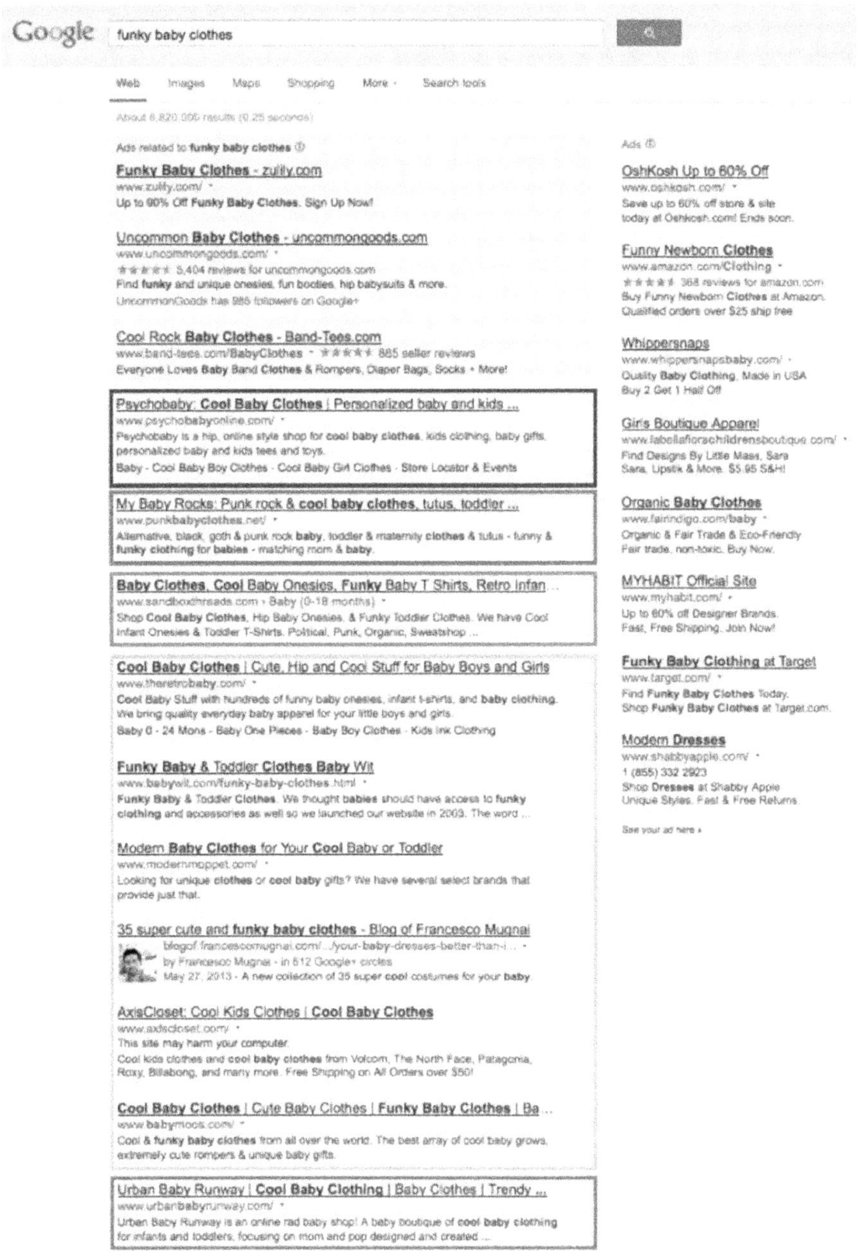
Google
funky baby clothes
Web Images Maps Shopping More Search tools
Ads related to funky baby clothes
Funky Baby Clothes - zulily.com
Up to 90% Off Funky Baby Clothes. Sign Up Now!
Uncommon Baby Clothes - uncommongoods.com
Find funky and unique onesies, fun booties, hip babysuits & more.
Cool Rock Baby Clothes - Band-Tees.com
Everyone Loves Baby Band Clothes & Rompers, Diaper Bags, Socks + More!
Psychobaby: Cool Baby Clothes | Personalized baby and kids ...
My Baby Rocks: Punk rock & cool baby clothes, tutus, toddler ...
Baby Clothes, Cool Baby Onesies, Funky Baby T Shirts, Retro Infan ...
Cool Baby Clothes | Cute, Hip and Cool Stuff for Baby Boys and Girls
Funky Baby & Toddler Clothes Baby Wit
Modern Baby Clothes for Your Cool Baby or Toddler
35 super cute and funky baby clothes - Blog of Francesco Mugnai
AxisCloset: Cool Kids Clothes | Cool Baby Clothes
This site may harm your computer.
Cool Baby Clothes | Cute Baby Clothes | Funky Baby Clothes | Ba ...
Urban Baby Runway | Cool Baby Clothing | Baby Clothes | Trendy ...
Ads
OshKosh Up to 60% Off
Funny Newborn Clothes
Whippersnaps
Girls Boutique Apparel
Organic Baby Clothes
MYHABIT Official Site
Funky Baby Clothing at Target
Modern Dresses

THE BENEFITS OF ORGANIC TRAFFIC

Now that we have to find and explore exactly is organic traffic, let's take a look at the benefits. The benefits are huge! Being able to get consistently ranked for organic traffic around terms that are relevant to your niche is very, very powerful. There are a lot of reasons why. So let's explore them.

It's FREE!

First and foremost, it's free! Once you get ranked organically, every time someone clicks on your website, you don't have to pay for that traffic. Pretty much all paid advertisements are based on PPC or Pay Per Click. So whether it's Facebook, Google, Yahoo or Bing, any time someone clicks on a paid advertisement, you as the advertiser have to pay the search engine for that click.

When you're getting ranked organically, it's free every time! You don't have to pay on a per click basis. In my opinion, this is by far the best strategy because it allows you to scale. Once you are ranked, you don't have to pay. It's a consistent potential source of revenue for your business going forward.

There are NO restrictions

When I say there are NO restrictions, what I mean is that how you lay out your website's home page is important from an SEO perspective. Meaning, your page structure and the way your site is laid out and displayed to the search engines is very, very important. But what you sell, how you sell it, how you collect names or what you're doing on the site after the fact, you're not restricted by Google, other than the fact that you need to have your page structured properly for SEO. But they can't say, "No, you can't sell that product" or "No, we don't like that opt-in offer".

Truthfully, if you're running PPC (Paid Per Click) campaigns, whether it's through Google, Yahoo or Bing, they can restrict what page you're sending the link in the paid ad. So if someone clicks a paid advertisement, the search engine has to approve the page you are sending the traffic to, which means you have to conform your website, product, opt-in offer, wording, even the structure of the link on your ad, to their requirements.

If you are getting ranked organically, you're simply following what Google tells you to do from an organic perspective or an SEO perspective. But they're not necessarily monitoring what your offer is or any of those details. You have none of the restrictions of paid advertising. Your only concern is making sure your home page is structured optimally to get the highest ranking on Google.

Set it and forget it

Another benefit of organic traffic is it's kind of a "set it and forget it". Once you understand and you get a site ranked organically for SEO, it's relatively easy to stay there.

Truthfully, Google, Yahoo and Bing are consistently changing the way they approve paid campaigns. So it becomes increasingly difficult to consistently monitor your different campaigns if you're running the campaigns for paid traffic. Whereas organic traffic, once you get ranked, it's much easier to stay there and have that process continually reap recurring benefits without consistent improvement or tweaks or monitoring. Which takes us to the next benefit of…

Scalable

Organic traffic is very scalable. Once you have a site that's ranked organically, you can do things that help push it up in the rankings. But you also have the ability to go after a bunch of different key terms with additional sites or additional pages. Organic traffic is very, very scalable because you don't have to spend as much time, effort and energy – and of course, money – to have those tangible results as you would with a paid advertisements strategy.

Let's take a look at these benefits a little bit deeper.

Free

So let's talk a little bit more about the fact that organic traffic is free. Once you build the website and have it ranked, the traffic comes to you at *no* cost. Any marginal cost with each additional visitor or traffic is zero.

Now you may have some costs if you have someone writing articles for you, or you have someone doing some different things to your site, there may be a small fee associated with that. And I certainly recommend not writing your own articles and other similar tasks, as you know from Book 1 of this series: *"Freeing Up Your Time – VA's, Outsourcing & Goal Setting"* (available on Amazon.com).

No Restrictions

Let's look at the benefit of no restriction a little bit deeper. When you have a site that is ranked organically around a specific keyword, you can choose to take whatever action with that visitor that you want.

So assuming that your SEO is correct and allows you to get ranked organically, whatever your offer or your strategy for monetization of that site really is up to you. Whether you're sending them to an affiliate offer or whether you're trying to capture a name or whether you're sending them to some sort of sales page, your strategy on your website that people find organically is really up to you and is not dictated by Google.

When we are talking about no restrictions, let's say you're running a PPC or a Pay Per Click campaign through Google, or even Yahoo or Bing, you not only have to have approved of the ad or the description that appears when the ad is displayed, but they also monitor and dictate the pages that you were sending them to.

So if you have ever run a PPC campaign, you know what I am talking about. You just don't have the full flexibility on how you're trying to monetize the visitors that you attract via your paid campaigns.

Once you get organically ranked, you can send your traffic to your page around pretty much any offer that you want. You're not relying upon Google telling you, "Sorry, we don't want to have a visitor see that page". You don't have this kind of restriction when it comes to organic traffic. And this is one of the biggest benefits of organic traffic.

Set it and forget it

Where we're talking about "set it and forget it", once your page is ranked you don't have to do much to keep it there. It really becomes the process of understanding and having a simple, laid out plan to consistently add content, very easily and very inexpensively, to allow you to stay in the organic rankings.

Scalable

Organic traffic is very scalable. The cost is minimal to add more sites – basically just the domain name and some additional content.

The biggest reason why it is scalable is simply the fact that, in order to go after more traffic, you simply build more websites around high-traffic keyword terms.

Remember, you're not paying per click, so building more websites does not cost you for the traffic.

WHAT IS SEO?

In this chapter we're going to explore the meaning of SEO. It is not something to be scared of! SEO stands for "Search Engine Optimization".

Most people know that by now, but a lot of people don't understand exactly what it can do.

There are a handful of important elements that make up good website – or On-site – SEO.

Good SEO is all about doing exactly what the search engines want you to do. SEO is actually relatively easy if you have a system and you understand what those pieces are and how to display your information in your site exactly how Google wants it laid out in the proper structure.

Off-site SEO requires a little more work and time.

Off-site SEO has to do with the process of building links, the process of your site aging. It's basically the credibility builder of your website.

How credible is your website? Google to other pages and activity about your website all across the web to see and monitor how relevant your site is around a particular keyword.

Keywords are the most important element to On-site and Off-site SEO.

There are a few important elements to keywords.

- Keyword Research

You have to understand what keywords are relevant to your business. A lot of people use a whole bunch of sort of related keywords for their business. But the key is to have keywords from which you can make money. You not only want keywords that you can rank for, that are relevant to your niche or your industry, but you also need to have keywords that are money keywords.

- Action Keywords

Action keywords are keywords that you rank for, that are relevant to your niche we are in receipt, and also that are money keywords. Think of these as specific actionable and buying types of keywords – not just general information keywords.

- Pick the Right Keywords

- Avoid "Keyword Stuffing"

A lot of people think that using the same keyword over and over and over again, without following the proper structure laid out by Google, is going to give them some sort of benefit – which is wrong! That strategy is called "keyword stuffing" – and Google may actually penalize you for this approach. Google can see what is relevant keyword usage and what is just this mind-numbing keyword stuffing strategy.

What is important is that SEO is not some sort of mystical strategy that is super complex. It is actually relatively easy because Google doesn't really high but they want you to do. Google wants you to make their job easy. They want to provide relative content to those who use their search engine. What we do as marketers when we take a proper SEO approach on our on-site SEO on our webpage to get ranked organically is exactly what Google tells us to do, meaning we have our keyword usage in the right location.

So that is SEO and a nutshell; it's not more complicated than that. Next we're going into the exact specifics.

HOW TO OPTIMIZE YOUR ON-SITE SEO

In this chapter were going to talk about how to optimize your on-site SEO. Remember, in the previous chapters we have talked about the two main elements of SEO or Search Engine Optimization. Briefly, we have on-site SEO which are the elements that you influence on your particular website, and off-site SEO being all of the things that you do to optimize your site off of your site – on other websites, social bookmarking sites, etc. In this chapter we're focusing on things that you are going to be doing to the elements of on-site SEO for your webpage.

Let's talk about some of the more significant elements.

Domain Name

The domain name is the first place that you can optimize. Google is going to look to either your domain name for your extended URL structure to have the keywords that you are going after.

Website

Next is the general website itself and the title of the page.

H1 Tags

The H1 tags or Header tags.

Meta Page

The meta page descriptions and the meta page keyword content.

Keywords in the Content

The keywords in the actual content of the webpage.

This is where a lot a people think they should start – having keywords in the content – but it goes much, much deeper than this. The initial four elements – domain name, website title, H1 tags and meta page – are sometimes actually more important than just the keywords in the content. In fact, successful SEO is built around, not choosing just one or two or three or four elements out of the five – it's all about doing *everything*. Having perfect on-site SEO and all of the elements that Google is looking for is what is going to prove to be successful.

HOW TO OPTIMIZE YOUR ON-SITE SEO DOMAIN NAMES

If you can select domain names with the keywords or phrases for which you want to rank, this will absolutely help your rankings.

Let's say you have to different websites that we are trying to rank. One of them has the actual keyword that we are going after in the root domain – in the part of the domain between the "www" and the ".com". If the keyword is contained in the root domain, it is looked at as more significant than if the keyword is not contained in the root domain. If everything else is considered equal – all of the on-site and off-site elements were exactly the same – the site with the keyword term in the domain will be seen by Google as more significant.

It is a very important strategy to have the keyword term in the domain name. If it's not in the domain, the next best place that it could be is in the Extended URL. The Extended URL is anything after the ".com". For example, www.mybusiness.com/keyword. This is an example of an Extended URL.

So if you have it in the domain, that is best. If you don't have it in the domain, it needs to be in the Extended URL.

HOW TO OPTIMIZE YOUR
ON-SITE SEO WEBSITE TITLE

Website titles are used to identify what your website is all about. Website titles are easy to identify because they are located at the top of pages within the browser. You can edit the website title in the Header of your HTML code.

This image is an example of my website KipPiperBooks.com. As you can see, "Kip Piper Books | Small Business Books to Improve Your Business and Make Money Online!" is the website title. So this website title includes the keyword or the key term that I should be going after for this particular site.

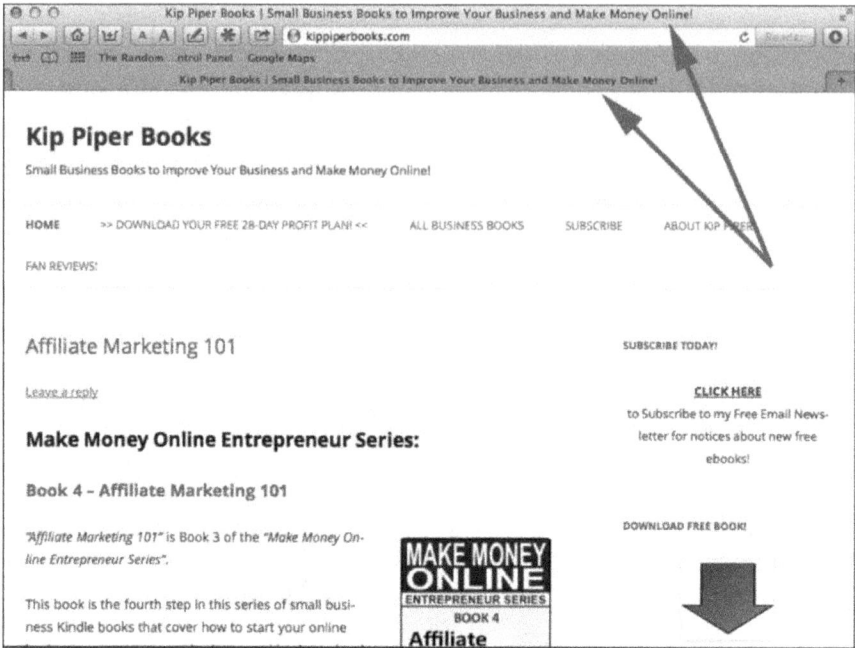

So to check how your website title appears, look at the top of your browser, as indicated by the arrows in the image above. Your title is a job description of your website and you want to have your keyword included in the title of your website.

HOW TO OPTIMIZE YOUR ON-SITE SEO H TAGS

"H Tags" is simply the abbreviation for the term "Headline tags".

There is a hierarchy of H tags. Typically they are:

<h1>Heading</h1>

<h2>Heading</h2>

<h3>Heading</h3>

<h4>Heading</h4>

<h5>Heading</h5>

<h6>Heading</h6>

So let's make the concept of H tags or Header tags a little simpler. It is usually the key phrase that summarizes or is a title of what's contained on the webpage below it in the form of content.

Let's look at an example of an H1 tag. Below is a page from a client's website and the H1 headline tag is "Revealed: The Exact Step-By-Step System to Correctly Creating a CE Marking Technical File". Notice that it's in bold and on top of content that is directly related to the key terms in the headline. And you notice that the content below it is optimized for the key phrases "CE Marking" and "Technical File".

So speaking of content, let's now discuss meta keywords.

HOW TO OPTIMIZE YOUR
ON-SITE SEO META KEYWORDS

Meta keywords are the main keywords that you want your site for a particular page to rank for.

You can edit these meta keywords in your website's HTML code or by using Google Optimizer, if you have a WordPress website.

Below is an example of the little piece of HTML code. Now not to worry! You do not have to be an HTML coder! The important thing is to take a look at the portion outlined in red. This is what your meta keywords coding looks like.

You have: meta name="keywords" and then the content are the exact key terms that we're going after for this particular site.

```
'all' />
<link rel='stylesheet' id='contact-form-7-css' href=
'http://www.phoenixtechnicalgroup.com/wp-content/plugins/contact-form-7/includes/css/styles.css?ver=3.4.2' type='text/css' media=
'all' />
<link rel='stylesheet' id='social-widget-css' href=
'http://www.phoenixtechnicalgroup.com/wp-content/plugins/social-media-widget/social_widget.css?ver=3.6' type='text/css' media='all'
/>
<meta name="description" content="We are a certified woman-owned small business (WOSB) that provides quick, capable, cost-effective
technical and engineering services through an international network. " />
<meta name="keywords" content="Phoenix Engineering Services: Design and Post Design Services Compliance and Verification, Design
Verification Plans, Drawing Conversion to Electronic Format, Safety Assessment, Risk Assessment, International Standards
Verification, Reliability Prediction, RGT Planning" />
<script type="text/javascript">/* <![CDATA[ */ var SHRSB_Globals = {"src":
"http:\/\/www.phoenixtechnicalgroup.com\/wp-content\/plugins\/sexybookmarks\/spritegen_default","perfoption":"1","twitter_template"
:"%24%7Btitle%7D+-+%24%7Bshort_link%7D+via+%40Shareaholic","locale":"0","shortener":"google","shortener_key":"","pubGoSocial":0,
"pubGoKey":""}; /* ]]> */</script><script type='text/javascript' src=
'http://www.phoenixtechnicalgroup.com/wp-includes/js/jquery/jquery.js?ver=1.10.2'></script>
<script type='text/javascript' src='http://www.phoenixtechnicalgroup.com/wp-includes/js/jquery/jquery-migrate.min.js?ver=1.2.1'>
</script>
<script type='text/javascript' src='http://www.phoenixtechnicalgroup.com/wp-content/themes/atahualpa/js/DO_roundies.js?ver=0.0.2a'>
</script>
<script type='text/javascript' src=
'http://www.phoenixtechnicalgroup.com/wp-content/plugins/wp-mailto-links/js/wp-mailto-links.js?ver=1.2.0'></script>
<script type='text/javascript' src='http://www.phoenixtechnicalgroup.com/wp-includes/js/comment-reply.min.js?ver=3.6'></script>
<script type='text/javascript' src=
'http://dtym7iokkjlif.cloudfront.net/media/js/jquery.shareaholic-publishers-sb.min.js?ver=6.1.3.8'></script>
```

Now, you do not need to know exactly how to do this. What is important for you to know is that meta keywords are an important element to SEO.

You don't need to know how to code meta keywords because there are easy tools that will place these meta keywords in the right location in your website.

So remember that meta keywords are important when you're building out your site and getting your site ranked with the search engines.

HOW TO OPTIMIZE YOUR ON-SITE SEO KEYWORDS IN THE CONTENT

Up to now we've talked about different elements of on-site SEO structure. We've talked about the domain, the title, the header tags, and the meta keywords. Now we're going to talk about the keywords in the content.

Having keywords in your content is one of the most important aspects of SEO. In my opinion however, it is not *the* most important but it is important.

Keyword Density is the measurement of keywords as a percentage of the entire content piece.

For example, if you have a 500-word article on a webpage and you use your keyword 5 times in that 500-word article, what is your keyword density? In this example, it is simply 1%.

Another way of saying it is Keyword Density is the number of times that your keyword is used as it relates to the total of number words in the article or webpage.

Density is *not* the most important element. It's not really important whether it's 2% or 7%, even though many of us to see those numbers recommended.

It is much more important to focus on writing (or having your VA write) Quality Relevant Content. Of course, make sure you're keywords are used when writing this Quality Relevant Content.

As for the percentage, make sure your Keyword Density is at least 2% but no more than 7%. Remember, if it's more than 7%, your article will be seen as keyword stuffing. Also, it is difficult to write a good quality article that has a keyword density of more than 7%. Why? Because it just won't read or flow very well.

So whether you shoot for 2, 3, 4 or up to 7%, the important thing is to use the keywords in a relevant manner so it makes sense in the article, and that the article is clear with high-quality content.

HOW TO OPTIMIZE YOUR OFF-SITE SEO

In this chapter were going to discuss how to optimize your off-site SEO. Remember on-site SEO are all the things that you do *on* your website – to structure your content, have the proper keywords, etc.

Off-site SEO pertains to everything that happens or relates to our website on all of the other websites out there on the Internet. Offsite SEO is relevant and important because Google looks to your website's activity or links back to your website as a way to rate the relevance of your website.

In other words, the more your site is referenced or linked to from other websites, Google looks at that as evidence that your website is relevant since other people are linking back to your website.

So off-site SEO refers to the elements that are out there on the Internet and pointing back to your website and increasing your ranking within the search engines.

Off-site SEO uses other websites to give your site more credibility by making your site the center of influence for your keywords. It makes your website more relevant in the eyes of Google.

So here are some ways to do this…

HOW TO OPTIMIZE YOUR OFF-SITE BACKLINKS

What is a Backlink?

A Backlink is simply a link on another site that links back to the site you are trying to get ranked.

So if you own "www.thebestwebsiteever.com", the more times other websites out there have links back to "www.thebestwebsiteever.com", the more powerful it is.

HOW TO SET UP BACKLINKS

There are a couple of automated tools to help setup back links to your site. The two that I have found to be the most effective are:

Onlywire.com
   http://www.onlywire.com
Dmoz.org/help/submit.html
   http://www.dmoz.org/help/submit.html

However even with these automated tools, not all backlinks are created equal. Dmoz is rated lower because there are a ton of links pointing out from their site and few that point in.

So the more influential a site is, in that there are a lot of links pointing to that site (or backlinks it has), the more valuable that site's link to your site is going to be.

Also the less backlinks a site is giving out, the more valuable its link to your site may be.

Another valuable backlink is when you receive a link from a site that is relevant to your niche. In other words, if a link to your website is on that niche-related site, the more powerful that link will be viewed in the eyes of Google – much more powerful than a link from a general social bookmarking site.

For instance, if I have a link on Twitter back to my website or if there is a link on a niche-specific site (which can even be one of my other websites) that's very relevant to my niche, Google will look at the link on a niche-specific site as being more powerful and more relevant than my link on Twitter.

Now do you get all stressed out and think you need to go out there and only get relevant links? No. The strategy really should be to get as many links as possible. So you want to go out and generate a lot of different links. What is important is that you understand that not all links are created equal, and to get both less relevant and more relevant backlinks in your strategy to get as many backlinks as possible.

SOCIAL MEDIA LINKING

Let's discuss Social Media Linking, or Social Bookmarking. It really is the easiest place to generate links. It's the easiest because there are a lot of different sites out there and everyone has profiles. Let's break it down.

Good linking:
- LinkedIn
- Google Plus
- YouTube
- Flickr

The social media sites above tend to have more high-quality, relevant links as it pertains to social media linking. There are a couple of reasons why.

One is that Google loves Google Plus and YouTube. Why? Because Google owns these. So obviously Google will provide more relevance to sites that they own over sites that they don't.

Also on LinkedIn, for instance, doesn't have as many general links. Yes, LinkedIn is a huge site with a ton of profiles, but the links or more strategic simply due to the nature of LinkedIn and the people on it. So the links on LinkedIn are more relevant and considered good linking.

You notice I'm not calling them "great links". This is because social media linking is never going to be considered great links in the eyes of the search engines. I would consider a "great link" as a link from within the forum or within a site that is a very reputable and relevant site directly targeted around my niche.

A "good link" as pertains to social would be on the sites listed above.

"Not so good linking" would be from Facebook and Twitter. Notice I didn't call them "bad links" because there's no such thing as a bad link – just less relevant.

Ultimately, Google looks at the total number of links back to your website. So you're not going to be able to generate a massive number of backlinks using only highly targeted linking strategies, such as, going after links that are laser-focused within your niche. So it's important that you go after some of please other bigger, larger, more general sites, such as Facebook and Twitter. The links are still relevant, and you still want to accumulate them.

ARTICLE SYNDICATION

Now we are going to discuss article syndication.

Ezinearticles.com

The biggest player is Ezinearticles.com (http://www.Ezinearticles.com). This is a site that contains and lists articles from across all different niches. The goal is to have an article with links back to your website. Ezinearticles is look at in the eyes of Google as fairly relevant because articles that are listed on this site with links back to your site are unique articles. Google likes that! So it's not just sharing a link, there is content around that link.

Squidoo.com

Next is Squidoo.com (http://www.Squidoo.com). This is another great place to have articles syndicated with links back to your site.

Hubpages.com

Finally, there is Hubpages.com (http://www.Hubpages.com), also a great place to have articles syndicated with links back to your site.

Obviously there are other article syndication resources out there, but Ezinearticles.com, Squidoo.com and Hubpages.com are three of the biggest players.

We have talked about a variety of ways of creating backlinks to your site, from social media sites to websites to article syndication. The thing to remember in the end is that there are no bad links. All links are good links. Your focus in your off-site SEO link-building strategy encompasses all of these different methods – going after highly targeted, niche-specific sites, going after good social media sites, going after not so good links or bigger social media sites, and going after article syndication.

TRAFFIC GROWTH MODEL

In this chapter we're going to talk about the Traffic Growth Model.

What is it? And why is it the most successful strategy of generating consistent organic traffic in and around your niche for multiple key terms?

The Traffic Growth Model is the strategy of building multiple sites around less competitive key terms, and building these sites to be laser-focused to rank for those specific key terms.

As an example, instead of building one site around a set of 10 keywords that are searched a total of 10,000 times a month, which is extremely hard to rank for, you build 10 simple sites – one site laser focused per key term, with each key term searched 1,000 times a month – and rank each of these sites.

Here is how it looks:

Versus

So on the bottom, you are going after 10,000 total searches, trying to rank for all of those key terms within one website, which is very hard to do.

What you want to do instead, as shown on the top, is to create a single website for each keyword. You are still going after the same 10,000 searches, but it is easier to rank a single site on a specific, laser-focused keyword than a website with tons of keywords.

Why do you want to go after the strategy at the top instead of the strategy at the bottom? There are a couple of reasons.

First, in the top example, the reason you are going after just 1000 searches is not because they have less search volume. Obviously, you want as much as search volume as possible. But generally speaking, these lower search volume terms are not only laser focused around your niche, but more importantly, they have significantly less competition.

So you know exactly what search by more going after, and you know what you are up against in the kind of competition you have for your key term.

This is where a lot of people go wrong when they are thinking of SEO. They tend to have an egotistical view that, if they do all of their SEO right, they will get ranked just because they consider themselves or their product so great. Honestly, that is not the case.

Efficient and effective marketers that leverage SEO understand that competition is huge. You want to go after terms that you can most easily rank for and are most relevant to your business.

That's exactly what this strategy is: build multiple sites around multiple key terms, instead of just building one site around that same group of key terms and traffic.

ADDITIONAL BENEFITS OF THE TRAFFIC GROWTH MODEL

There are some additional benefits around using the Traffic Growth Model than just getting that search volume.

Test different marketing messages

One of my favorites, it allows you to test different marketing messages. Remember, the Traffic Growth Model is all about building specific sites around specific key terms. So in other words, when you build a site, everything – from the domain to all of the content on the site to the title – is all focused around the specific key term that people are searching for. So you know when people visit that site, they found that site 99.9% of the time from entering that search term or that key term into Google.

So what does this allow you to do? It allows you to have a specific marketing message on that website geared towards that exact search term that people are searching for. This is quite powerful! You can target that marketing message laser focused around that key term.

Less Risky (not putting all of your eggs in one basket)

I love strategies that are less risky, especially when it comes to SEO. So instead of putting all these super competitive key terms and all of your marketing strategy into one website, instead you go after less competitive terms with a bunch of smaller websites.

What's the benefit? Let's say one of these smaller websites doesn't get ranked for some reason. With the Traffic Growth Model, you still have nine other chances to go after all of that traffic. Now you know if you stay up to date and you follow a specific strategy, you will have a greater likelihood of being ranked.

So it's very important, no matter what niche you go after, that you have multiple sites going after multiple keywords, instead of just having one big massive site and hoping it gets ranked.

Rank MUCH faster and easier

You get ranked much faster and it is so much easier. Anytime you're going after less competitive terms, not only is it easier, but you get ranked faster. Speed of implementation is everything in starting and building an online business. Being able to be ranked faster means having tangible results much faster. This is a huge benefit of the Traffic Growth Model.

Owning more than one spot on Google's top 10

The Traffic Growth Model allows you to own more than one of the top spots in Google on the first page. This is HUGE!

Sometimes when you were building out niches and using this specific Traffic Growth Model, you will find that you'll have 1, 2, 3, sometimes 4 of your sites ranked on the first page of Google for that exact term. It is absolutely amazing, and it works!

Earlier we talked about the differences between the number of clicks on the first position, the second position, and so on. If you have more than one site ranked on the first page of Google, the chances of your site getting clicked go through the roof!

So the Traffic Growth Model is really important and provides huge benefits that you can't get with the traditional SEO strategy.

NICHE BUILDER

So we have explored the Traffic Growth Model. Honestly, the concept of having a lot of different sites around specific keywords that are relatively low in competition and have sufficient traffic is really great in theory. It's a powerful strategy, but typically in the past it just took a lot of time. It took an incredible amount of effort to create all of these different sites around specific keywords. That's where Niche Builder can streamline that process.

Niche Builder (http://kippiperbooks.com/NicheBuilder) is a tool that simplifies the Traffic Growth Model by putting all the tools you need into one easy-to-manage place. With Niche Builder, you can implement the strategy on a larger scale in one easy-to-manage software tool. It allows the Traffic Growth Model to be executed very quickly and efficiently.

(Yes, this is a shameless plug for Niche Builder [http://kippiperbooks.com/NicheBuilder]. I have used many of the other tools on the market, and I find Niche Builder to be simply the best and most comprehensive. So for this book and the entire series, I will be referring to Niche Builder as my tool of choice.)

So let's look at little bit closer at Niche Builder.

Niche Builder has the most comprehensive keyword research tools on the market.

- It allows you to do specific general keyword research.
- It also has a direct API with Google that pulls back general searches and related search terms around your niche.
- It allows you to identify what the search volume is.
- It allows you to identify the number of competing pages, which is very important.
- And to build on that, the keyword research tool also allows you to analyze the difficulty of ranking for a specific key term.

Here is a screenshot of the detailed analysis of the specific key phrase "cheap baby clothes". It pulls back the results on the first page of Google for this key phrase. As you can see below, there are 10 sites listed. These are the top 10 sites listed on the first page of Google.

The green "no" areas above tells you that these sites are **not** using that specific key phrase in the domain, the website title, the header tags, nor the description. If you remember, we have identified these as being four of the most important on-site SEO components.

So this tool allows us to very quickly make educated decisions on what keywords you want to go after based on the level of competition.

Frankly, this strategy – understanding exactly how competitive a particular keyword is, not only in the number of competing pages but specifically the first 10 results and Google for particular search term – allows you with confidence to go forward and build sites around that key term. You know the competitor information up front.

This way you can go after the low hanging fruit in your niche. It allows you to rank much quicker and much easier, with a very detailed picture from the start.

In my opinion, this keyword research element is by far the most important component of SEO. Without this information, you are really going into it blind. Having a clear understanding of exactly how many searches there are (the potential of getting ranked for that term), as well as the competition (how difficult it is to rank for that term), before you actually start doing the work or building the site, gives you a huge advantage over your competition.

BUILDING A WEBSITE IN NICHE BUILDER

Building a website is extremely easy with Niche Builder. The steps are clearly laid out within the software.

It's important to not concern yourself with the visuals of the website to start with. It doesn't matter what it looks like if no one is seeing it yet. Many people are so concerned with what the website is or how it looks and opt-in offer.

The most important thing in SEO is getting the site ranked.

Because if you're not getting the site ranked and no one is seeing it, then who cares what it looks like?

So the initial focus on your website is all about content and getting the site ranked.

Start out with 3 to 5 pages of content on all of your new website projects. Eventually you're going to want to build that out to 5, 10, 15 pages, depending on how competitive that particular term is. But first, always start out with at least 3 to 5 pages of content.

BACKLINKING IN NICHE BUILDER

Niche Builder allows you to backlink very easily. It has a sophisticated integrated SEO function. You simply follow the steps, fill out the fields, and when completed, click "Submit".

The important thing is to first get your website up and filled with content, then you can start building your backlinks.

INCREASING RANKING

One of the important components of Niche Builder is it allows you to monitor and manage your rankings very easily.

Remember you always are looking to increase your rankings and making sure you are ranked at the top of search engines for the particular key terms and phrases you're going after.

There are a couple of different ways to increase your site's ranking.

Content

In Google's eyes, content is king – even more so than backlinks. While backlinks and everything we do in SEO is important, content is very important to Google.

You need to add a piece of content every 2 to 3 days to help your site rank faster.

The most important part of the process when you are monitoring your rankings is in the initial phases – when you were going out and trying to get your site ranked for the first time or trying to move them up in the rankings – your sites require much more attention. Once a site has been around for a little while, older and established, and is ranked, it requires less attention.

However, when we talk about increasing your rankings and building out additional content every 2 to 3 days, it's important that you understand that this is in the beginning phases when you're trying to move your site up the rankings.

Purchasing SEO

We also try to get more backlinks by purchasing SEO in combination with adding content.

Niche Builder offers excellent quality and reasonably priced content and

SEO services. You can also purchase content and SEO services through freelance websites, and then simply enter the content and SEO information into your Niche Builder website.

TRAINING IN NICHE BUILDER

Niche Builder has an extensive and easy to understand training process built right into the software. In addition, their customer support is exceptional. They want to be sure that you fully understand and are able to take full advantage of everything the software has to offer. I have even had personal, live one-on-one training from one of their support specialists in order to understand a function.

Be sure to go through their training so you can realize the full potential of what the Niche Builder software has to offer.

TRAFFIC GROWTH MODEL ON STEROIDS

Now HERE is the real power behind the Traffic Growth Model: When you build a website around a specific key term, build only ONE page – a squeeze home page – around that term. Then build one subpage PER ADDITIONAL KEY TERM under that squeeze home page. This strategy is what will get you MULTIPLE listings on the first page of Google for your chosen keywords!

This is how you do it.

As an example, let's say we are using the top 5 "baby clothes" keywords best suited for our niche, as identified using Niche Builder. These 5 top keywords have at least 1,000 monthly searches and less than 300,000 other sites optimizing for these keywords. They are:

- Cheap baby clothes = 8,100 searches / 159,000 competitive websites
- Vintage baby clothes = 4,400 searches / 76,700 competitive websites
- Wholesale baby clothes = 4,400 searches / 253,000 competitive websites
- Unique baby clothes = 2,400 searches / 137,000 competitive websites
- Funky baby clothes = 1,480 searches / 89,000 competitive websites

Your first website will have the Home page optimized around the keyword term "cheap baby clothes". This page should include:

- Website domain name "Cheap Baby Clothes"
- Page title "Cheap Baby Clothes
- Headline "Cheap Baby Clothes"
- Short (less than 1 minute) sales video (either a video of you or a PowerPoint presentation with a voiceover) structured with:

- Identify your visitor's problem
- Offer a solution
- Benefits to the solution
- Why you are the expert
- Call to action (fill out form with name and email to receive free bonus report, etc.)
- One or two paragraphs of content (300-500 words – 500 is best), positioned below the video, which is optimized for "Cheap Baby Clothes"
- Call to Action repeated
- Online form where the visitor can enter their name and email address to receive their free bonus report (or whatever you decide to give away). Once they submit their name and email, they are added to your subscriber list and are redirected to your main website.
- Meta tags and meta description optimized for "Cheap Baby Clothes".

NEXT:

As a SECOND page to your website, create another squeeze page structured exactly like described above (except for the domain name), BUT optimized for your second keyword term "Vintage Baby Clothes".

As a THIRD page to your website, create another squeeze page structured exactly like described above (except for the domain name), BUT optimized for your second keyword term "Wholesale Baby Clothes".

As a FOURTH page to your website, create another squeeze page structured exactly like described above (except for the domain name), BUT optimized for your second keyword term "Unique Baby Clothes".

As a FIFTH page to your website, create another squeeze page structured exactly like described above (except for the domain name), BUT optimized for your second keyword term "Funky Baby Clothes".

That completes your first website.

For your second website, build the Home page around your second keyword term "Vintage Baby Clothes", structured just like the Home page described above.

For your second, third, fourth and fifth pages, optimized each one in turn for the keyword terms "Cheap Baby Clothes", "Wholesale Baby Clothes", "Unique Baby Clothes" and "Funky Baby Clothes".

For your third website, build the Home page around your second keyword term "Wholesale Baby Clothes", structured just like the Home page described above.

For your second, third, fourth and fifth pages, optimized each one in turn for the keyword terms "Cheap Baby Clothes", "Vintage Baby Clothes", "Unique Baby Clothes" and "Funky Baby Clothes".

For your fourth website, build the Home page around your second keyword term "Unique Baby Clothes", structured just like the Home page described above.

For your second, third, fourth and fifth pages, optimized each one in turn for the keyword terms "Cheap Baby Clothes", "Vintage Baby Clothes", "Wholesale Baby Clothes" and "Funky Baby Clothes".

For your fifth website, build the Home page around your second keyword term "Funky Baby Clothes", structured just like the Home page described above.

For your second, third, fourth and fifth pages, optimized each one in turn for the keyword terms "Cheap Baby Clothes", "Vintage Baby Clothes", "Wholesale Baby Clothes" and "Unique Baby Clothes".

This is how the overall structure looks:

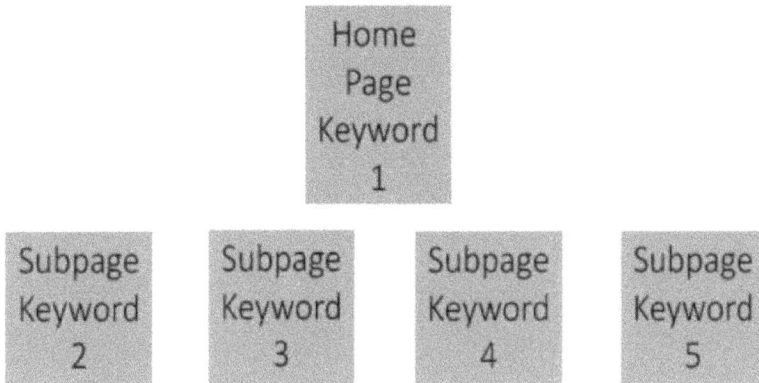

Home Page Keyword 1			
Subpage Keyword 2	Subpage Keyword 3	Subpage Keyword 4	Subpage Keyword 5

There are a few IMPORTANT RULES YOU MUST OBSERVE for this "steroids" model to work:

Simply replace all of the "baby clothes" related keyword terms in the example above with your chosen keyword terms.

Every single page on every single website MUST have unique content. You can write the content for the first website and its 5 pages, then hire someone to rewrite each of them as new content. Or you can hire someone (or multiple someone's) to write all of them as unique content.

Fivrr.com (http://www.kippiperbooks.com/fivrr) is a great source for short 300-500 word content at just $5-$10 per piece.

THERE IS NO MENU showing the subpages from the Home page. They each stand alone. You don't need a menu, and a menu would just confuse the visitor. The important thing is that Google will find them and separately rank them.

You CAN use the same – or slightly modified, if appropriate – video for every Home page and subpage.

For this two work, you MUST have at least 3 sites for 3 keyword terms and include all of the Home pages and subpages. However, 5 sites are better and will get you ranked faster. As mentioned above, you can add to these sites and pages as you find other strong marketable keyword terms.

Yes, this "Traffic Growth Model on Steroids" does take work and a little expense. I promise you – put this "Traffic Growth Model on Steroids" into place, and you will see results! After all of the work you have already done, not taking this step can mean the difference between success and potential failure.

THIS IS THE MISSING LINK for successful affiliate marketing!

BONUS MATERIALS

Below is the link to this book's bonus material. I have developed this tools from my own experience as well as compiled from tools I have used from various training courses I have taken.

The mind map is built in XMind software. You can download a free version of XMind from http://www.xmind.net.

The item is also available as a PDF.

Strategic_Plan_SEO_Organic_Traffic.xmind
http://www.kippiperbooks.com/make-money-online/book05/Strategic_Plan_SEO_Organic_Traffic.xmind

Strategic_Plan_SEO_Organic_Traffic.pdf
http://www.kippiperbooks.com/make-money-online/book05/Strategic_Plan_SEO_Organic_Traffic.pdf

MORE KINDLE BOOKS BY KIP PIPER

Ultimate Affiliate Marketing with Blogging Quick Start Guide
    http://www.kippiperbooks.com/UltimateGuide

Make Money Online Entrepreneur Series:

Below are just a few of the books in this series. To browse the entire series, go to:
    http://www.kippiperbooks.com/makemoneyonlineseries

Book 1 – Freeing Up Your Time – VA's, Outsourcing & Goal Setting
    http://www.kippiperbooks.com/book1
Book 2 – Your Core Business, Niche & Competitors
    http://www.kippiperbooks.com/book2
Book 3 – Blogs & Emails: Your Link with Your Customers
    http://www.kippiperbooks.com/book3
Book 4 – Affiliate Marketing 101
    http://www.kippiperbooks.com/book4
Book 5 - Driving Traffic with Organic SEO
    http://www.kippiperbooks.com/book5
Book 6 – Power of Email Marketing
    http://www.kippiperbooks.com/book6
Book 7 – Quick Income Formula with Advanced Affiliate Marketing
    http://www.kippiperbooks.com/book7
Book 8 – List Building with Facebook
    http://www.kippiperbooks.com/book8
Book 9 – List Building with Twitter
    http://www.kippiperbooks.com/book9
Book 10 - List Building with LinkedIn
    http://www.kippiperbooks.com/book10

ONE LAST THING…

As you can probably tell from my writing, my intention is to inspire and support more people to build a better financial future. It's a tough economy today, and I think personal growth in the field of small business is more important than ever before. Even though I have well over 20 years of experience as a successful small business owner and online entrepreneur, I don't have all the answers. In fact I'm still learning myself, I just have my own opinions, experiences and a passion for being my own boss to guide me through life.

Thank you purchasing my eBook and for taking the time to read it. I hope you enjoyed it and found value within its pages.

If you did I would really appreciate your support by taking the time to write a review for me on Amazon. Reviews really help the authors you enjoy to get noticed in a crowded marketplace, and it would allow me to continue writing the books for this series and other business books.

Please visit the URL below to let me know your thoughts:

http://kippiperbooks.com/book5

All of my books are offered completely FREE on the launch and I want to reward loyal readers by offering my new books to them FREE of charge when they are released.

So please visit my website KipPiperBooks.com and either download your free copy of *"28-Day Small Business Profit Plan: The Quick Start Guide to Business Success"* or just sign up to my newsletter in order to be kept informed when the next release is due. I hate spam, so I promise I won't share your information with anyone – not for love nor money!

Good luck! I wish you every success in your personal and business endeavors.